WABI
SABI

WABI SABI

—

Finding Beauty in Imperfection

Oliver Luke Delorie

STERLING ETHOS
New York

STERLING ETHOS
New York

An Imprint of Sterling Publishing Co., Inc.
1166 Avenue of the Americas
New York, NY 10036

ISBN 978-1-4549-3254-3

Distributed in Canada by Sterling
Publishing Co., Inc., c/o Canadian
Manda Group, 664 Annette Street,
Toronto, Ontario M6S 2C8, Canada

For information about custom editions,
special sales, and premium and corporate
purchases, please contact Sterling Special
Sales at 800-805-5489 or specialsales@
sterlingpublishing.com.

Manufactured in China

10 9 8 7 6 5 4 3 2 1

sterlingpublishing.com

MIX
Paper from
responsible sources
FSC® C104723

CONTENTS

INTRODUCTION

J apanese monks describe *wabi sabi* as "reaching an appreciation of what is really important in life by eliminating everything that is not essential."

In the film *American Beauty*, wabi sabi is an old shopping bag twirling in the wind, minutes before the first snow of the season. The narrator is nearly in tears glimpsing the place where two equals one.

Even though there is no definition for wabi sabi—if it could be defined it wouldn't be wabi sabi—I have, with great care, endeavored to describe the indescribable (as I like to call it), a task I believe I share with those seeking to understand the world around them, and an enlightening

process evident in every form of art and construction I see. All creative acts are proof to me of this desire to make manifest below the glory of above.

This attempt to distill the wisdom of the delightfully asymmetrical invisible world dancing beyond the veil only became possible once I had embraced the inevitable discord, disarray, and disfunction hiding in all I see, hear, think, feel, touch, do, and say. Once acknowledged, mind-bending complexity gave way to profound simplicity and led me to realize that wabi sabi is indeed the spirit of change; the passing of time; the acknowledgment, appreciation, and acceptance of the transient and temporary nature of all things in the cycle of life.

May you find in this book a philosophy that helps you understand your ever-changing mind, body, and spirit. I warmly wish the spirit of wabi sabi washes over you as you watch your relationships, creative practice, work, hobbies, and projects change over time.

Oliver Luke Delorie

1

WHAT DO YOU SEE?

You have a multitude of senses
with which to manipulate your experience.
Technique and caliber are up to you.
Use not only your eyes to see.

LOOK CLOSER

———

At first glance, mold and mildew are unappealing—
hideous, even—to the untrained eye. When encountering
life in all its guts and glory we are often far from
charmed; it can be hard to see the beauty in the
seemingly rotten and repugnant. Yet focusing on the
basic functions of a person, place, or thing will
undoubtedly reveal its intrinsic nature and ultimate
value. Every day we are given ample opportunity to
glimpse the inherent beauty in all things.
So the next time you find yourself repulsed
or repelled, simply look closer.

The dance of duality

The opposite of every noun in your life is lurking
in the shadows with a trick up its sleeve. Whether you
see it or not is of no consequence; the contrastingly
charged essence of what you believe is patiently waiting
to trip you up or sabotage your best-laid plans.
But knowing is half the battle, so print your name
on wabi sabi's dance card and await your turn.

ORDER vs. CHAOS

———

Order is defined as the arrangement or disposition
of people or things in relation to each other according
to a particular sequence, pattern, or method.
Chaos is defined as complete disorder and confusion.
When both seem alive and well, as is often the case, why
not accept the inevitable push-and-pull and appreciate
the magnificence of each? Doing so will bring you one
step closer to grasping the principle of wabi sabi.

66 I see beauty in the bent, the rotting, the decayed, and the shattered. I find splendor in things most would find terrifying. I think damaged things are exquisite, because I know they are just like me. They are not ruined forever; things that are broken have a funny way of being fixed and turning out better than before. 99

Jordan Sarah Weatherhead,
author of *Naked Truth*

Reality is in the eye of the beholder

Reality is a human concoction. If perception is fact, then real life is up to you; you are free to believe what you see, for you see what you believe. Seek beauty and you shall find it, as you would buried treasure beneath the sea, hitherto lost for centuries. What is appealing is personal; its defining grace and virtue a solo mission. Thus, reality is hereby objective, is it not?

ILLUSION

———

Unfortunately, truth does not garner the same
popularity and fanfare as its sexy cousin fantasy.
Truth is pure, clear, and succinct. Fantasy is free flowing,
mystical, and dreamy. Truth is solid; fantasy fluid.
Who doesn't want to get lost in the buoyant ethereal
dimension of limitlessness when truth is so hard-edged
and definite? The secret to finding beauty in
imperfection is to appreciate the intoxicating feelings
delusion readily offers, while simultaneously
acknowledging them as simply such.

2

KEEP IT
SIMPLE

All things being equal, the simplest
solution is the best. Would you agree?
If not, give it some thought.
If not, keep reading.

SIMPLE IS BEAUTIFUL

Simplicity is clarity and perfection, and as a result impermanent, thanks to our human inability to sustain the thoughts, feelings, and actions belying it. This is why lack of sophistication can be so beautiful and elegant. The more we strive to attain it, the more it eludes us. Perhaps those who risk sliding down the slippery slope seeking to revel in its beauty may in fact be the only ones who glimpse the blissful place where nothing else matters.

Clutter is distraction

———————————

Consider the fact you may be a slave to the things you own. Yes, stuff comes in handy; there is a reason you keep what you accumulate. Your snow shovel and winter tires are useful; every time you play golf, you don't want to rent clubs and a cart. And twenty types of occasions require twenty pairs of shoes. Unfortunately, expending time, money, and energy to maintain, store, and regularly replace your cherished clutter only distracts you from finding beauty in the well-made tools of your trade. The notion of wabi sabi suggests using it or losing it.

Understated usefulness

———

Before you throw it out, ask yourself:
How does this old milk can add to my enjoyment of life?
Could I clean it, polish it, paint it, or repurpose it?
Everything at one time served one purpose or another.
What would it take to appreciate and fall in love with
your old milk can again? A little introspection
might reveal or rekindle the reason you
acquired it in the first place.

EFFORTLESSNESS

Water wears down rock and delicate weeds eke their way through cracks in the sidewalk to commune with the warmth and light of the sun. With no other purpose than pure existence, every detail of nature seems intentionally on purpose. Although easier said than done, adopting a similar approach to work and play can usher in bottomless relief once you let life unfold in its own time and in its own way.

Decision-making

Instead of impulsively rushing headfirst toward
the most attractive option in front of you, why not
look at the issue from differing angles: What seems
the perfect solution? What would heaven suggest?
What would hell say? Be patient with yourself,
because nothing will ever be perfect. That's how
you decide to find beauty in imperfection.

The purpose of our lives is to be happy.

——

The Dalai Lama

The answer is in the opposite

When faced with discord, chaos, and confusion,
the path of least resistance is seldom apparent.
Acceptance of what is happening is beyond difficult
to grasp, let alone hold onto. One way to get a peek
at what may be the truth of any matter is to look
where you have not. What are you refusing to see?
What possibility would devastate you to acknowledge?
Herein lie the clues to the answers you seek.

3

THE
POWER OF
APPRECIATION

Acknowledge what is good in your
life, and stress and worry will evaporate.
Few other psychic strategies yield
such impressive results.

Rustic aesthetic

Worn, tattered, and torn objects are nothing more
than expressions in, and of, the timeline of life.
Inevitable and unavoidable, we are forever surrounded
with crumbling proof of fated existence. Nouns in
every form mutate in their own way, according to their
own schedule. Is this not irresistibly bewitching?
Count yourself lucky when you glimpse the magnificence
of time unfolding as it does right before your eyes.

FUNCTIONALITY

In the old days, stuff was made to last.
Thanks to planned obsolescence, manufacturing
consumer goods with intentionally short lifespans,
we not only clutter up our lives with useless
junk—and in so doing further distance ourselves
from wabi sabi—we are encouraged to forget
how such thoughtfully produced objects can
remain functional for decades, if not centuries.
What could last a lifetime?

66 Be in a state of gratitude for everything that shows up in your life. Be thankful for the storms as well as smooth sailing. 99

Dr. Wayne Dyer, author and speaker on spiritual growth

Your old car

———

Getting from A to B is what is important.
Let not color, year, make, or model matter to
your nosy neighbors. Shun any shame you have
held for your old clunker in the past, or how you
or others judge it now, for the secret to wabi sabi
is finding inner calm in function over form.
If it ain't broke, don't fix it.

TRANSFORMATION

Recognize the ability of everything you see, think,
taste, touch, smell, and imagine to adapt and reorder
itself in the process of perpetual evolution/dissolution.
Nothing stays the same. Even solid rock is focused on
its crustaceous-snail-slow affair of transmogrification.
Knowing life is in a constant state of flux will
help you see the binary code informing all
things at hummingbird-wing speed.

Repurpose

———

A garden in a teacup; an oil-drum barbecue;
a school bus tiny house on wheels. The options are
endless and defined only by what we deem possible.
Seeing possibility in the objects and tools around
us is a rare ability worthy of special attention
and due care. Turn something inside out and
upside down and see what happens.

Harmony

———

Disharmony runs rampant in society because discord runs rampant inside of humans. Some say harmonizing inner (and thus outer) disquiet is the secret to enlightenment. As long as round-the-clock symmetry eludes us, gently seeking-it-but-not-seeking-it seems to be the most direct way to wabi sabi. Once the kids are grown up, your records are a hit, and you've climbed every mountain, what else is there to do? Unearth the charm buried in imperfection, of course.

APPRECIATION

———

Expressing your appreciation for a gesture of
kindness, compassion, or patience has a powerful
effect on those involved (even if the recipient of the
appreciation is your trusty can opener or a favorite pair
of scuffed leather boots). The act of recognition itself
creates a dynamic vacuum effect that both connects
and binds you with an intangible yet meaningful
respect for life. Thank every blessing in disguise.

Meditate

———

If only you could quiet the Indy 500 rat-race track in your head. If only you could calm the inner voices urging you to get on with anything but what you're attempting to get on with. If only you could relax and loosen up and just be. Meditation could be described as the practice of sitting, waiting, and loving everything you're hating, on the road to wabi sabi.

4

TRUST TIME

Do we have a choice?
When all things operate on a
space-time schedule (and we
have not the tools to tinker),
we best go with the flow.

The meaning of life

You are far from perfect, yet are in a divine
position to derive any degree of significance from
your time on Earth you wish. Just as trying to pin a tail
on wabi sabi will forever be fraught with folly, defining
and describing what gives your life meaning may forever
elude you. When this inevitably happens, know that you
are the essence of life realizing itself and you may
find the beauty of the imperfect inside of you.

NOTHING LASTS

If everything existed eternally we would have
nothing to grieve over, nor would we ever celebrate
joy or success again. Few ups and downs would matter,
if exist at all. Taking comfort in the depth of endlessness,
though frightening at first, can be like sailing the sea
of tranquility while contentedly raising your glass and
toasting the sunset at the end of the day. The journey
is the destination; getting there is half the fun.

There is no end

—

Trillions of eons prove nothing is finished.
Is the universe made only of love, as some philosophers argue? If so, love will last for an eternity, as it will never find its polar resolution. If it ever did, every atom in the multiverse would simply evaporate. What if love is not at the core of infinity? Then we have to wait twice as long.

Patience

Calm and composure. Without these qualities we would not wait around for our gardens to grow, our investments to mature, or ever get to where we want to go. Nor would rot, repairs, or asymmetry ever take our breath away. Our perception of time and space is ambiguous, and our understanding limited, so if ever you find yourself unable to sleep, desperate in your desire to catch a glimpse of wabi sabi, calm your mind and your body and be patient. Do this and you will see it everywhere.

> **"** We don't stop playing
> because we grow old.
> We grow old because
> we stop playing. **"**

———

George Bernard Shaw, Irish playwright

WATER

———

If wabi sabi took shape or form, water would
be a contender. Fluid and responsive, water yields
to its surroundings and flows freely without judgment
or definition. Essential, abundant, and overflowing,
H_2O does not have an agenda, nor does it stress about
perfection or purpose. It just goes with the flow.
An ocean of acceptance of imperfection.

Stillness

———

Chase a butterfly and it will fly away.
Be still and it will land on your shoulder.

5

LET GO

There is a reason we are so powerless.
Life regularly demands us to let go.
Why do we argue with the highest
form of parental guidance?

Be nonjudgmental

The next time the opportunity to evaluate a person or experience confronts you (roughly every minute of every day) see if you can stop yourself before your instinctual split-second appraisal of delight or disgust kicks in and derails any sort of calm acceptance of however it/he/she is behaving. Peace and serenity tend to show up bearing gifts when you let things be and change at will. The next time you climb a hill, scale a rock face, or have a rooftop view, what do you see? And how do you feel about it?

A fistful of sand

Ever try holding sand in a clenched fist?
Not the best container. Few metaphors describe
the fundamental quintessence of holding on versus
letting go in such a simple, yet ingenious, way.
When you see that impermanence, flux, and
rollercoaster are fitting synonyms for life,
you open your hand, palm side up. This is how
to hold, carry, and care for what you cherish.

TRANSIENCE

Fleeting are the moments in time when we truly
trust in the unfolding of existence. If the principle of
perennial transformation is suffusing all matter, surely
we can enjoy the comfort in, and of, unending renewal
and maintain our faith that healing takes place and
shines a spotlight on the dark places in and all around
us. Then, only, may we perhaps find the beauty hiding in
fated faults and failings. Don't be afraid. It's just a delay.
A karmic frolic. Let it all go.

Let it be

If destiny prevails, do we have a say in the matter?
In our ability to (we believe) choose what, when,
where, and how, we are contented and satisfied;
though only for a short time, for one question
remains: Why? This heart-wrenching, soul-stirring,
mind-blowing, one-word question that loves to
leave our lips has perplexed eons of generations.
Let it be. Resistance is futile.

" Mindfulness is simply being aware of what is happening right now without wishing it were different; enjoying the pleasant without holding on when it changes (which it will); being with the unpleasant without fearing it will always be this way (which it won't). "

James Baraz, coauthor of *Awakening Joy*

PEACE

———

Conflict and chaos are imperfection personified,
whereas peace is unconditionally patient. Cultivating
calm contributes a stillness that may only be found when
immersed in such activities as looking into the glassy
mirror of an undisturbed puddle and becoming one with
the magnificence of the moment. All at once, you become
aware that sustaining grace among all confusion and
commotion requires nothing but an effortless devotion
to your inner candle flame. Never let it flicker,
regardless of what goes on around you.

" For peace of mind, resign as general manager of the universe. **"**

Larry Eisenburg, science-fiction writer

THE FORCE

━━━━━━━

While Kermit was a thoughtful puppet and Miss Piggy the most boisterous, Yoda's misshaped noggin held light years of knowledge within it. Upon seeing the disappointment in his pupil's eyes due to the latter's lack of progress and thus growing impatience, the light-green-carpeted guru counseled young Skywalker with sage advice: Against the force you rail; this is why you fail. In the event we heed the words of this respected philosopher, we will "use the force" rather than the other way around.

The path of
least resistance

Water goes where gravity tells it to, and electricity
finds the shortest way from A to B. Choosing a path with
fewer sticks and twigs, rocks and roots will open doors
of possibility beyond which the beauty of the world
blossoms, for it existed long before you did, and will
endure long after you leave. Stop bushwhacking your
way through life. Put down the machete and marvel
in the magic of a rainbow fractal in a soap bubble
while you're arm-deep in dishes.

6

WHAT MATTERS MOST?

Defining and clarifying the purpose of our lives is such a monumental task that, without understanding our intentions for it, all else is meaningless.

VALUES

———

If you are to ever commune with your
unfathomable spiritual core, or learn what flicks
your switch and makes you tick, you must query:
What matters to me? Without conscious awareness of
your innermost workings, any whisper of wabi sabi
will drift away like a blossom on the breeze, never to be
seen of or heard from again. That's no way to live,
especially if you crave kinship with divinity.
What matters the most to you?

Relationships

If friends are worth more than gold (and your family
somehow made their way to the podium) everyone parts
with a medal in the grueling triathlon of life. Without
physical, emotional, and spiritual connection to other
human beings, we would whither on the vine and shrivel
up into nothing quicker than you can say "empty" (which
is how life seems without intimacy and platonic
companionship that come from attachment to other
life-forms infused with semiconsciousness).

" Freedom is not overcoming what you think stands in your way. Freedom is understanding that what is in your way is part of the way. "

Guy Finley, self-help philosopher
and spiritual teacher

PLAY

We play for no other reason than to express ourselves
and find joy. How we apply our tools and toys in search
of the meaning in each moment is a marvelous metaphor;
wabi sabi is just waiting around the corner with a smile
on its face waiting to pounce and surprise us with
delight. When our playful intentions take a left turn,
or result in brilliant innovation or dazzling realization
(as is often the case when we mess around with
abandon), we often see the perfection in all things,
regardless of the expectations we initially held so tightly.

Creativity

We create to communicate. Exploring alternatives
and experimenting in any way is the secret to original
and artistic breakthroughs that not only change the way
we see the world, but also how the world sees itself.
Visionary, enterprising, and imaginative, everyone
is creative and bursting with immeasurable ability,
given the chance to discover what they find beautiful in
this speculative adventure wherein we seek divine unity
with the nebulous notion of wabi sabi. There are no rules.

LOVE

——

There are as many words for this sacred
experience of affection, adoration, and devotion as
there are for snow. And as any poet knows, falling in
love while snow is gently falling is just about as good as
it gets. Given the temperament of love in all its forms,
comparing our experience of love to an encounter with
wabi sabi is fitting; we are frequently encouraged to see
the beauty in a partner's early-morning hairdo; the soft
marshmallow center within a misshapen exterior; or the
sensitive inner child quietly anticipating reassurance
beneath a posturing grown-up facade.

7

CELEBRATE TRADITION

There are seven billion (and counting) ways to honor and respect yourself. Learn from your mistakes and celebrate your success.

WAY OF THE TEA

The traditional Japanese tea ceremony known as
chanoyu, *sado*, or *ocha*, and literally steeped in matcha
(powdered green tea), owes its origins to Zen Buddhism.
Considered one of three classical Japanese aesthetics
(along with *kōdō*, the art of incense appreciation,
and *kadō*, the art of flower arranging), the Japanese
tea ceremony is infused with the practitioner's sacred
devotion to the ancient art form and represents
a fundamental—principled—longing to understand
pure simplicity within the complexity of modern life.

Personal history

———

Even though families often fight with feudal friction, your history is rife with ancestry; full of stories and skeletons and quirks-a-plenty. Yet the juicy fruit of significance languishing in the bygone days of long ago can only be found in the overgrown orchard you call your past. Memories tend to pile up like boxes of unsorted photos, so untie any knots of guilt or regret and lay to rest the mortal negativity that clobbered your tender soul back when you were only years removed from the place wabi sabi calls home. Your blemished past is history and your future is an unfinished mystery, figuratively and patiently waiting for a new coat of paint.

RITUALS

We cherish and cling to customs and traditions, observing and performing prescribed steps at set times in our lives in order to rekindle and relive a special experience or celebrate a person, place, or thing that is meaningful to us. Faith in our established actions breathes nuance into our celebrations and instills patience into our observances, and so it is in these formal and informal practices that we can cultivate a heartfelt reverence for wabi sabi (even if it inspired Murphy's Law to crash the party).

66 Traditional wisdom
is long on tradition and
short on wisdom. 99

———

Warren Buffet, business magnate,
investor, and philanthropist

Pilgrimage

———

The search for spiritual and/or moral significance
has for eons inspired treacherous travels that may not
always have succeeded in reaching desired conclusions
(whether that be lasting enlightenment or actual arrival
at one's intended destination). Like wabi-sabi-inspired
alchemy, when we begin a spiritual journey we expect
to trudge through graphite lead and bask in the
glimmering gold once we cross the finish line. Yet it
turns out the port of call is more metal-like, and
every pitch and toss of the voyage is silently glistening
with gold if we choose to watch and listen.

8

PERFECTLY IMPERFECT

If perfection existed, nothing would.
It is this friction that binds everything together,
for good or for ill. Nothing is symmetrical.

DETAILS

Experience and understanding multiply in direct relation to how close up and intimately you engage in, and with, a situation. If the devil is in the details, angels and saints are keeping watch as you delve into the depths of specifics. Permit careful consideration of any condition, and you will fashion the skeleton key that unlocks the door to the room where the secrets of eternity are lying low. The greater the capacity of your inner zoom lens, the deeper down the rabbit hole you can go.

Let the light in

We would not know light if dark didn't exist.
Without hope, the faith in possibility, we would not
see beyond the bend; the probability that fear would
overtake us would loom so large that it inevitably
would (and does). It's risky to gamble against seemingly
invincible odds and trust that in every obstacle lies
the promise of potential. Sometimes this is all we have
to go on, so the next time you are hopelessly staring
face-to-face with a problem (your inability to see
the relevance in or of something) find the cracks
in the wall where the light is shining through.

" Peace is not the absence of conflict. Peace is the ability to handle conflict by peaceful means. "

Ronald Reagan, former president

JOY

Far from joy, at the extreme opposite end of the emotional spectrum, is misery; the lackluster state of heartbreak and grief that is at first terrifying and depressing, but has lessons to teach. Class is now in session. What can we learn from suffering? We learn we are not alone. We learn to clarify what matters. We learn that nothing lasts, and this too shall pass. Pleasure is not joy, nor is excitement. Joy is blissfully wiping away tears in the depths of despair; experiencing ecstasy in anxiety; and finding sweet solace in weakness and deficiency.

Healing

———

Prolonged exposure to wabi sabi has not one
side effect. Rather, this nonverbal condition is
curative and therapeutic in every way to those who
should imbibe of its restorative and health-giving
blessings. What could be more beneficial than
finding peace and purpose and benevolence
and meaning in every meddlesome mishap
and pesky difficulty? There is nothing more
your mind, body, and soul could ask for.

VULNERABILITY

─────

We all feel unsure and powerless at times. The issue arises when you judge the strength and/or weakness of your response to said stimuli. Verdicts only keep you from what you desire: an open mind and heart to accept the world as it is. Luckily, the path you seek is littered with bread crumbs, and because birds are fluent in wabi sabi, the sweet sourdough morsels will be waiting for you when you reach the trailhead. You will never get lost in the forest of life as long as you bend with the forks and marvel in the magic. Be at ease with (your) weakness, and birds will eat out of your hand.

COURAGE

———

It takes guts to follow your heart and enjoy the cool breeze or warm wind. The sweetest fruit can be found beyond the thorny fight for freedom and our prejudices toward what we encounter in our quest for perfection. Believe in the effortless happiness of pursuit and you will earn the pluck required to let go of the insecure fear of your inability to grasp the gist of what's going on. One of the perks is X-ray vision. Angelic child's play.

Virtue

To make a virtue of something means to derive benefit or advantage from submitting to an unwelcome obligation or unavoidable circumstance. In other words, accepting the inevitable imperfection in all things is vital if we desire happiness. When living the wabi-sabi life, we are encouraged to see the diamond in the rough; to cherish the treasures we unearth; and to celebrate the possibilities hidden beneath the surface. Finding elegance and grace in imperfection is essential, for until we can even temporarily embody this virtue, we will lack a deep and meaningful relationship with all things.

9

RADICAL ACCEPTANCE

Having faith in how things happen
will welcome serenity into your life.
Whatever happens, happily deal with it.

PEACE OF MIND

———

Peaceful thoughts are a choice, like most habitual
thinkings. Given your umpteen years of experience on
Earth (and thus your exposure to countless opportunities
to be gracefully present in the moments that matter)
is it not time to make inner peace a priority? All the
clarity and compassion and patience you seek spring
and sprout from this blissful, undisturbed state of mind.
Aside from unconditional love, the only other purely
personal pursuit worth focusing on is this.

66 We have so little faith in the ebb
and flow of life, of love, of relationships.
We leap at the flow of time and resist in
terror its ebb. We are afraid it will never
return. We insist on permanency, on
duration, on continuity; when the only
continuity possible in life, as in love,
is in growth, in fluidity, in freedom. 99

Anne Morrow Lindbergh, writer

Self-acceptance

Without self-worth, we are rudderless ships headed for the rocks; putting our hulls, sails, crew, and cargo in danger. Our journeys downstream are fraught with unseen perils, so unless we signal the drawbridge keeper in time, or have a PhD in celestial navigation, we are risking our way to work and/or play. At times we all feel insignificant and inconsequential, though the truth is we are what we believe ourselves to be, and belief is the best guarantee. Build yourself an inner lighthouse to light the way and guide you the rest of your days.

PROCESS

———

Neither beginnings nor ends are perceptible.
Naturally this leaves us empty-handed. Wabi sabi
is the process of process, and the clock is timeless
and runs nonstop, whether we like it or not. If we
want to go for a swim, we have to get our feet wet, but it
doesn't end there. Raisin fingers are par for the course;
bell-bottoms for disco dancing. Any attempt to define
or describe what you find dangling at the end of
the ebb and flow yo-yo only results in further
equivocal questions. Process is unpredictable.

SOLITUDE

Though we may be surrounded with kinfolk,
we cannot ignore the fact we only have ourselves
to love and blame and to talk to about it. Over time,
time alone proves to lead to the sublime theory professed
in this book, so if you are already a card-carrying
member of the solo crowd, you may have a vague inkling
of what is going on here. The rest of us would do
well to listen to our inner voices once in a while;
a pursuit that requires privacy, peace, and the
absence of other stillness-seekers.

Self-improvement

The quest for self-knowledge and understanding
is often a quiet one; inward-focused and reflective.
What are we seeking? Surely, communion with our idea
of who and/or what cosmic divinity is. But down on
Earth there are more trivial matters to attend to;
like how do we get along with others? How can we
be more gentle and loving in the words we speak not
only to ourselves, but to the people we say we love?
How can we be more productive and creative? Why is
life so hard? The key to all of these questions lies
in a wave; a smile; a buzz; a song; a dream;
a whisper: You are perfect as you are.

CONCLUSION

You don't need permission to follow your inner knowing; that is the beauty of living an imperfect life. Free yourself from judgment about what you and others regard as true or beautiful or pure or right. Marvel in amazement at everything that happens. Stand in awe of every single second. Scrape off the rust and wash off the mud.

Relax as if you are a drop on your way to the ocean, knowing fear and doubt and separation become irrelevant the moment you get home. Unconditional permission is mandatory if you seek to be blessed by the boundless beauty in disguise surrounding you.

Let innocent magic and wonder wash over you as you become one with this place. Let the sun shine its light on your face and on all your surroundings, so they may be celebrated as is. Now integrate into infinity and you will indeed live a wabi-sabi life.

Both transient and lonely, permanent and popular, when it comes, the supreme rapture of this intoxicatingly fleeting connection, you will experience the moment you touch the imperfect purpose of reality, and you will fall deeper in love with the bona fide truth that "nothing lasts, nothing is finished, and nothing is perfect."

Recommended reading

Adams, Julie Pointer. *Wabi-sabi Welcome*, Artisan Books, 2017

Gold, Taro. *Living Wabi Sabi—The True Beauty of Your Life*, Andrews McMeel Publishing, 2004

Juniper, Andrew. *Wabi-sabi—The Japanese Art of Impermanence*, Tuttle Publishing, 2003

Koren, Leonard. *Wabi-sabi: For Artists, Designers, Poets & Philosophers*, Imperfect Publishing, 2008

WholeLiving.com

Picture Credits